Mary

Written by
Christine Virginia Orfeo, FSP

Illustrated by
Julia Mary Darrenkamp, FSP

Pauline
BOOKS & MEDIA
Boston

Nihil Obstat:
Reverend Thomas Buckley, STD, STL

Imprimatur:
✠ Seán Cardinal O'Malley, O.F.M. Cap.
Archbishop of Boston

March 30, 2007

Library of Congress Cataloging-in-Publication Data

Orfeo, Christine Virginia.
  My first book about Mary / written by Christine Virginia Orfeo ; illustrated by
Julia Mary Darrenkamp.
     p. cm.
  Originally published: c1996.
  ISBN 0-8198-4861-1 (pbk.)
  1. Mary, Blessed Virgin, Saint--Juvenile literature. 2. Mary, Blessed Virgin,
Saint--Apparitions and miracles--Juvenile literature. 3. Rosary--Juvenile
literature. I. Darrenkamp, Julia Mary. II. Title.
  BT607.O74 2007
  232.91--dc22

2007011759

English translation of the Apostles' Creed and Doxology by the International
Consultation on English Texts (ICET).

Published by Pauline Books & Media, 50 Saint Pauls Avenue,
Boston, MA 02130–3491.

Printed in U.S.A.

www.pauline.org

Pauline Books & Media is the publishing house of the Daughters of St. Paul,
an international congregation of women religious serving the Church with the
communications media.

1 2 3 4 5 6 7 8 9   11 10 09 08 07

Contents

THE LIFE OF MARY

God Promises
to Send a Savior

A very long time ago, God created the first man and the first woman. God loved them very much! They were God's special friends.

Then one day, our first parents said "No" to God. They committed a sin by disobeying God. How sad and sorry they felt after that! But God didn't want them to be sad. He promised them, "I will send you a Savior. He will help you become my friends again."

As time went on, there were many Jewish people living in the land of Israel. They believed in the one true God. God sent them holy men called prophets. The prophets told everyone that the Savior would come. The prophets said, "Believe God's promise! God will send a Savior. The Savior will free us from sin. A young woman will be his mother."

Mary Is Born

God waited a long time before he sent the Savior. The Savior would be God's own Son! The Jewish people waited and waited for the Savior to come. Joachim and Ann were a good Jewish couple. They also waited for the Savior. They lived in a town called Nazareth.

Joachim and Ann had been married for many years. But they didn't have any children. For a long time they had asked God to give them a baby. Then one day, God said, "Yes!" A beautiful baby girl was born. You can imagine how happy Joachim and Ann were! They named their baby Mary.

God had wonderful plans for Mary. He filled her with his love and friendship

from the first moment she existed. God
gave Mary special help to obey him all the
time. For her part, Mary
loved God with all
her heart. She
always said
"Yes" to
God.

Mary Goes to God's House

According to a story that has been handed down over the years, Ann and Joachim brought Mary to God's house. Mary was still a young girl when she went to live there.

The house of God was very big and beautiful. The house of God was called the Temple. Many people went to the Temple to pray.

Mary made friends with the other young girls who were living at the Temple. Together they learned more and more about God.

Mary prayed that God would send the Savior he had promised. Mary didn't know that God had chosen her to be the mother of the Savior. God hadn't asked her yet.

An Angel Visits Mary

The time finally came for God to send the Savior. First, God sent an angel named Gabriel to see Mary. The angels praise and serve God in heaven. They also bring God's messages to people on earth.

Gabriel said to Mary, "God loves you very much, Mary. God wants you to be the mother of his Son. The Holy Spirit will come to you. And you will have a baby and you will name him Jesus."

Mary told Gabriel, "Yes, I will please God. I will be the mother of his Son."

Then a wonderful thing happened! Jesus, God's Son, began to live and grow inside Mary as all babies live and grow inside their mothers. Jesus is the Son of God because God is his Father. Jesus is the Son of Mary because Mary is his mother. The name "Jesus" means Savior.

Mary Visits Elizabeth

When the angel Gabriel came to Mary, he also told her other good news. He said that Elizabeth, Mary's cousin, was going to have a baby boy, too! She would name him John. When John grew up, he would tell everyone about Jesus!

After Gabriel left, Mary hurried to visit Elizabeth. Elizabeth lived far away.

When she got to the house, Mary hugged Elizabeth. God had let Elizabeth know Mary's special secret. Elizabeth knew that Mary would be the mother of Jesus.

Elizabeth said to Mary, "God has blessed you more than any other woman!"

Then Mary thanked God with a beautiful prayer.

Mary helped her cousin Elizabeth very much. Mary is always ready to help us, too!

Joseph and Mary Go on a Long Trip

The name of Mary's husband was Joseph. He was a good man. He loved Mary, his wife. An angel told him that Mary was going to have a very special baby. The baby was God's own Son. God knew that Joseph would be a good father to Jesus.

Right before Jesus was born, Mary and Joseph had to go on a long trip. They had to go all the way to the town of Bethlehem.

It took many days to get there. The town was very crowded when Mary and Joseph arrived. Joseph tried to find a nice room for Mary. But he couldn't find any place for them to stay.

Then a kind man told Mary and Joseph about a cave. He said they could sleep in the cave that night. Mary and Joseph thanked the kind man.

Jesus Is Born

Mary and Joseph went to the cave. They were very tired that night. The cave was very poor. It was dark and cold. Cows and sheep were sleeping there, too.

During that special night, Jesus was born! It was the first Christmas! Mary held Baby Jesus. He was such a beautiful baby! She hugged him and kissed him.

Joseph made a little bed for Jesus. He put some hay in the wooden manger where

the animals used to eat.
Mary wrapped Jesus in
soft clothes. Jesus liked
his little bed of hay.

Then Mary and
Joseph prayed, "Thank
you, God our Father,
for sending us your Son,
Jesus! He is the Savior
of the world!"

Visitors Come from Far Away

On that first Christmas night, shepherds were watching their sheep. Suddenly, they saw a beautiful angel. The angel told them about the birth of the Savior. The shepherds were very excited. They ran to the cave. They knelt down to adore Jesus, their Savior.

Other visitors from far away came to see Jesus, too. Three wise men came from the East. They were called Magi.

The Magi wanted to see the Savior very much. A big bright star led them to Bethlehem. The Magi brought precious gifts for Jesus.

Mary and Joseph were happy to see the Magi. They welcomed them. Mary held Baby Jesus out to them. The Magi fell down on their knees before Jesus. They said, "We are so happy to see God's Son!"

Jesus had come to save the Magi. He had come to save the whole world. He had come to save us!

Mary and Joseph Bring Jesus to the Temple

Mary and Joseph brought Baby Jesus to God's house. They presented him to God.

Simeon, a holy man, was in the Temple. A holy woman named Anna was there, too. Simeon took Baby Jesus in his arms. Simeon said, "Blessed be the Lord! He has sent us his Son!"

Then Simeon looked at Mary. "You will have to suffer a lot," he told her. Mary was very quiet. She was thinking. Mary knew it wouldn't be easy to be the mother of God's Son. Mary loved Jesus so much. She knew that whenever Jesus suffered, she would suffer too. In her heart, Mary told God, "I will do whatever you ask. I know you will help me to be a good mother for your Son."

Jesus, Mary, and Joseph
Have to Run Away

A king named Herod was jealous of Jesus. He even wanted to kill Jesus.

One night, an angel warned Joseph, "Hurry up, Joseph! Take Jesus and Mary far away!"

Joseph told Mary what the angel had said. Mary quickly packed some things. Then she wrapped Baby Jesus in warm blankets.

That night, Jesus, Mary, and Joseph left Bethlehem. They hurried to a faraway land called Egypt. It was a long trip. But God helped them and kept them safe.

Jesus, Mary, and Joseph stayed in Egypt for awhile. Then an angel spoke to Joseph again. The angel said, "You can go back home now. Jesus will be safe."

Joseph and Mary took Jesus and went to live in the town of Nazareth. They were a very happy family. We call them the Holy Family. They loved God and one another very much.

Mary and Joseph Find Jesus Again

Jesus was a very good boy. He was loving and kind to everyone. He helped his mother, Mary, with the housework. Joseph was a carpenter. He taught Jesus how to make tables and chairs. When Jesus was twelve years old, Mary and Joseph brought him to the Temple. A special feast day, the Passover, was being celebrated there.

The Holy Family prayed in the Temple. When it was

time to go home, Jesus stayed behind. But his parents didn't know it. Mary and Joseph looked all over for Jesus. They couldn't find him anywhere.

Finally, they found Jesus in the Temple. Mary asked Jesus why he had made them worry so much. Jesus answered, "I have to do the work of my Father in heaven." Mary didn't understand what he meant, but she prayed about it for a long time afterward.

Joseph Dies
after a Good Life

Joseph worked hard, and he took good care of Mary and Jesus. Then one day, Joseph died in the arms of Jesus and Mary. He had always trusted in God, and he had a holy death.

Jesus took extra good care of his mother after that. He knew how much she missed Joseph.

Jesus worked hard in the little carpenter's shop. He was glad to help others. Jesus fixed things and made new furniture for people.

Jesus and Mary were very happy together.

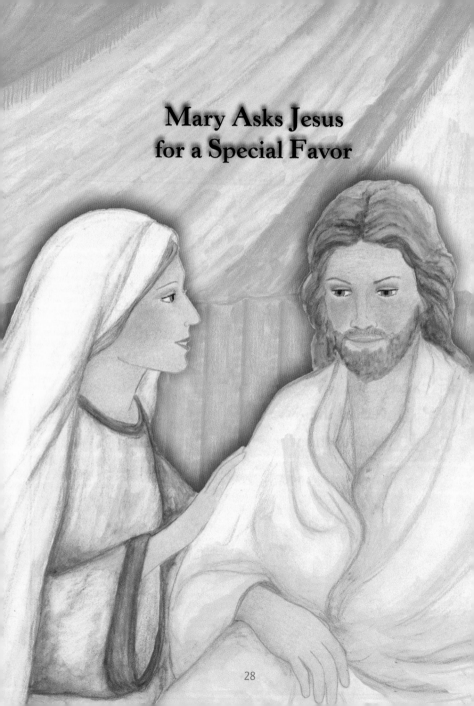

Mary Asks Jesus
for a Special Favor

Once, in a town called Cana, there was a wedding. Mary was invited to the wedding. Jesus and his friends were invited, too.

During the meal the people ran out of wine. Mary felt bad for that young couple. She didn't want their celebration to be spoiled.

Mary told Jesus, "The wine is all gone." She knew Jesus would help them, and she told the waiters, "Do whatever he tells you."

Jesus asked them to fill some big jars with water. Then he changed all the water into wine! That was a miracle! By changing the water into wine, Jesus showed everyone that he is God!

Jesus worked that first miracle because his mother had asked for his help. Just as the waiters did, we, too, should do whatever Jesus wants us to do.

Mary Follows Jesus

Jesus did many wonderful things! He taught everyone about our good Father in heaven. Jesus taught that we must love everyone. He showed us how important it is to pray.

Jesus cured sick people. He made blind people see. Jesus even raised dead people back to life!

Many people went to listen to Jesus. Mary followed Jesus whenever she could. She listened to Jesus. Mary was very happy to see all the wonderful things Jesus did.

Jesus Eats His Last Supper with His Friends

Jesus and his friends ate a special supper together. Jesus took bread and prayed. He gave the bread to his friends.

Jesus said, "Take this, all of you, and eat it. This is my body." Though the bread still looked like bread, it was now the Body of Jesus! Then Jesus took a cup of wine. He gave it to his friends. Jesus said, "Take this and drink it. This is the cup of my blood. Do this in memory of me." Even though the wine still looked like wine, it was now the Blood of Jesus!

At this Last Supper, Jesus gave all of us his own Body and Blood. We call the Body and Blood of Jesus the Holy Eucharist. At every Mass, the priest changes bread and wine into the Body and Blood of Jesus.

Mary Sees Jesus Suffer

Not everyone loved Jesus. Some people were jealous of him. They made up lies about Jesus. They hurt Jesus and made fun of him. Pontius Pilate, the governor, said Jesus would be put to death.

Jesus suffered very much! He had to carry a heavy cross. It was very hard to carry. It even made Jesus fall down in the street. But Jesus carried the cross to the top of a hill.

Mary followed Jesus to the hill. How sad she was to see him being hurt! Mary knew Jesus was suffering to save us from our sins.

Jesus Dies to Save Us

At the hill, the soldiers told Jesus to lie down on the cross. They banged big nails into his hands and feet. Then they stood the cross up. Jesus hurt very much! He offered his pain to free us from sin.

Jesus forgave everyone who hurt him. He was not angry. He did not complain. He kept on loving everyone—even the people who were hurting him.

Mary stood right under the cross. In her heart she felt all the pain that Jesus was feeling.

Jesus didn't want to leave his mother Mary all alone. Jesus saw his good friend John there. Jesus said to his mother, "There is your son." Then Jesus said to John, "There is your mother." From then on, John took care of Mary. Mary was a good mother to John. She is our mother, too!

Soon after, Jesus died. His good friends took him off the cross and buried him.

Jesus Is Alive Again!

After three days, Jesus came back to life! Jesus can do everything. He is God!

We call Jesus' coming back to life "the resurrection." We remember and celebrate Jesus' resurrection every Sunday by going to Mass. We celebrate Jesus' resurrection in a very special way on Easter Sunday.

Mary was so happy to see Jesus when he came back to life! We should all be happy, too. Jesus has promised that if we love and obey him, we will live with him forever. We believe Jesus because he is God!

Jesus Goes Up to Heaven

Jesus called his friends to a big hill. Mary, his mother, was there, too.

Jesus blessed Mary and all his friends. He told them, "Go and tell everyone about me. Baptize them in the name of the Father, and of the Son, and of the Holy Spirit. I will be with you all the time, even though you won't be able to see me."

Then Jesus went up to heaven. We call this "the ascension of Jesus."

Jesus Sends His Spirit to Mary and His Friends

Jesus didn't want to leave his mother and his friends alone. Before he went up to heaven, he promised them, "I will send you my Holy Spirit."

Then Mary and the friends of Jesus all prayed together. They prayed for nine days in a row. Suddenly, they heard a loud wind. Little flames of fire came over their heads! Jesus' Holy Spirit was coming to them! Mary remembered that day long ago when the Holy Spirit had come to her. That was the day she agreed to become the mother of Jesus. Now the Holy Spirit was coming to all Jesus' friends, and Mary would be their mother, too.

The Holy Spirit made them brave apostles. An apostle is a person who tells everyone about Jesus.

Mary is the Queen of all apostles. She brings Jesus to everyone.

Jesus sends his Holy Spirit to us, too. The Holy Spirit makes us strong and brave in following Jesus.

Mary Goes to Heaven and Is Crowned Queen

Mary prayed a lot after Jesus went back to heaven. She prayed that everyone would love and obey her Son, Jesus. Mary talked about Jesus to everyone who came to see her.

Mary watched the group of Jesus' followers grow and grow. The group of followers of Jesus is called the Church.

At the end of Mary's life, God did something special for her. He took Mary, body and soul, into heaven. We call this "the assumption of Mary." How happy Mary was to go to heaven! How happy Mary was to be with Jesus again!

Jesus is the King of the whole world. In heaven, Mary, his mother, is Queen.

Special Feast Days of Mary

January 1 ❀ Mary, Mother of God

February 2 ❀ Presentation of Jesus in the Temple

February 11 ❀ Our Lady of Lourdes

March 25 ❀ The Annunciation of Jesus' Birth

May 31 ❀ The Visitation of Mary to Elizabeth

July 16 ❀ Our Lady of Mount Carmel

August 15 ❀ Mary's Assumption into Heaven

August 22 ❀ The Queenship of Mary

September 8 ❀ The Birth of Mary

September 15 ❀ Our Lady of Sorrows

October 7 ❀ Our Lady of the Rosary

November 21 ❀ Presentation of Mary
in the Temple

December 8 ❀ Immaculate Conception of Mary

December 12 ❀ Our Lady of Guadalupe

Mary Comes to Visit

Mary has visited the earth many times since she went to heaven.

Here are some stories of her visits. They show us how much love and care Mary has for each of her children. Mary helps us to be good. She helps us to love God more and more.

Mary is our holy mother. Mary always prays for us. Whenever we need help, we can turn to our mother Mary. She will bring all our prayers to Jesus.

Our Lady of Mount Carmel

Many years ago, Mary appeared to a holy priest. His name was Father Simon Stock and he lived in England. Today we honor him as Saint Simon Stock.

Mary gave Father Simon a special gift. It's called a scapular because it is worn over your shoulders. (The Latin word for shoulder is *scapula*.) A scapular is made of two little holy pictures attached to two pieces of brown wool on strings. One picture goes in front and the other goes in back.

Mary takes special care of people who wear her scapular with love. She prays for them now and after they die.

The scapular is a sign of our love for God's mother. It is also a reminder and a promise of Mary's love for us.

Our Lady of Guadalupe

Another time, Mary visited the country of Mexico. She appeared to a good man named Juan Diego. Today we know him as Saint Juan Diego.

Juan was poor, but he loved God and Mary very much. One day Juan saw Mary on the top of a hill. She was wearing a long pink dress. Her head was covered by a blue veil decorated with stars.

Mary told Juan how much she loved him and his people. She said she was their heavenly mother! Mary even left a beautiful picture of herself on Juan's cloak to prove that she had visited him. She asked that a church be built on the hill.

Today there is a beautiful church there. It is called the Basilica of Our Lady of Guadalupe. The wonderful picture of Mary is still there for people to see. Many people visit the church to ask for Mary's help. Mary always prays for us to her Son Jesus.

Our Lady of the Miraculous Medal

Catherine Labouré was a young sister of the Daughters of Charity who lived in France many years ago. She loved Jesus and Mary very much.

Mary appeared to Sister Catherine. How beautiful our Lady was!

Mary said to Sister Catherine, "Have a medal made with my picture on it. Everyone who wears it will receive many blessings."

Sister Catherine had the medal made. We call this special medal the Miraculous Medal. The picture of Mary on the medal shows that Mary's hands are open. This reminds us that we receive God's blessings through Mary.

Around the picture are the words of this prayer, "O Mary, conceived without sin, pray for us who have recourse to you."

When we wear the Miraculous Medal, we find it easier to remember our heavenly mother.

Our Lady of Lourdes

Bernadette Soubirous was a poor girl. She loved God and his mother very much. Bernadette lived in a town named Lourdes. Lourdes is in the country of France.

Bernadette saw our Lady eighteen times! Mary told Bernadette, "I am the Immaculate Conception." This means that God created Mary free from all sin and filled her with his love and friendship from the first moment she existed. And Mary always said "Yes" to God.

A little stream of water began to flow from the spot where Mary appeared to Bernadette. Bernadette saw Mary over 150 years ago, but the stream of water is still there today. Sometimes sick people who drink from it are cured of their sickness.

Today many people go to Lourdes to pray.

We want to love Jesus and Mary very much. The Blessed Mother will help us to be good friends of Jesus, just as she helped Bernadette.

Our Lady of Fatima

Many years ago, our Lady visited a town named Fatima. Fatima is in the country of Portugal.

Three young children saw Mary that time. Their names were Lucy, Jacinta, and Francis.

Mary told the children to pray for peace. She asked them to pray the Rosary. She also asked them to offer God small "sacrifices." Sacrifices can be things that are a little hard for us to do. It can also be a sacrifice to give up doing something we would like to do. The important thing is to offer up our sacrifices out of love for God.

Mary told the children that we can all offer sacrifices to God so that bad people can become good. We can pray that people will be loving to each other. We can try our best to become like Jesus, just as Lucy, Jacinta, and Francis did.

Our Lady of the Rosary

Have you ever heard of the prayer called the Rosary? A very long time ago, Mary taught Saint Dominic how to pray the Rosary. Saint Dominic was a priest. He loved Jesus and Mary very much. He taught many people how to pray the Rosary.

The Rosary is a special kind of prayer. When we pray the Rosary, we think about the lives of Jesus and Mary. We think of the times when they were very happy or very sad. And we are glad to remember the wonderful things that happened to them. We call these different times in the lives of Jesus and Mary the "mysteries" of the Rosary. These "mysteries" are divided into four parts: Joyful, Luminous (meaning full of light), Sorrowful, and Glorious. You can find the names of the mysteries on pages 62–63.

As we think about the mysteries, we say prayers on a special chain of beads called rosary beads. You can find these prayers on pages 60–61.

THE PRAYERS OF THE ROSARY

The Sign of the Cross

In the name of the Father, and of the Son, and of the Holy Spirit. Amen.

Our Father

Our Father, who art in heaven, hallowed be thy name. Thy kingdom come, thy will be done on earth as it is in heaven. Give us this day our daily bread, and forgive us our trespasses, as we forgive those who trespass against us. And lead us not into temptation, but deliver us from evil. Amen.

Hail Mary

Hail Mary, full of grace, the Lord is with you. Blessed are you among women, and blessed is the fruit of your womb, Jesus. Holy Mary, Mother of God, pray for us sinners, now and at the hour of our death. Amen.

Glory

Glory to the Father, and to the Son, and to the Holy Spirit. As it was in the beginning, is now, and will be for ever. Amen.

After the Glory at the end of each of the 10 Hail Marys, we may also say the prayer that Mary taught the children when she appeared at Fatima.

The Prayer Mary Taught Us at Fatima

O my Jesus, forgive us our sins, save us from the fires of hell. Lead all souls to heaven, especially those most in need of your mercy.

The Apostles' Creed

I believe in God, the Father almighty,
  creator of heaven and earth.

I believe in Jesus Christ, his only son, our Lord.
  He was conceived by the power of the Holy Spirit
    and born of the Virgin Mary.
  He suffered under Pontius Pilate,
    was crucified, died, and was buried.
  He descended to the dead.
  On the third day he arose again.
  He ascended into heaven,
    and is seated at the right hand of the Father.
  He will come again to judge the living and the dead.

I believe in the Holy Spirit,
  the holy catholic Church,
  the communion of saints,
  the forgiveness of sins,
  the resurrection of the body,
  and the life everlasting. Amen.

Hail, Holy Queen

Hail, holy Queen, Mother of mercy, our life, our sweetness, and our hope. To you do we cry, poor children of Eve; to you do we send up our sighs, mourning and weeping in this valley of tears. Turn then, most gracious advocate, your eyes of mercy toward us; and after this our exile, show unto us the blessed fruit of your womb, Jesus. O clement, O loving, O sweet Virgin Mary.

The Mysteries of the Rosary

The Joyful Mysteries

1. The Angel Announces to Mary
   that She Will Be Jesus' Mother
2. Mary Visits Elizabeth
3. Jesus Is Born
4. Jesus Is Brought to the Temple
5. Jesus Is Lost and Found in the Temple

The Mysteries of Light

1. Jesus Is Baptized
2. Jesus Changes Water into Wine at Cana
3. Jesus Announces God's Kingdom
4. Jesus Is Transfigured
5. Jesus Gives Us His Body and Blood at the Last Supper

The Sorrowful Mysteries

1. Jesus Prays and Suffers in the Garden
2. Jesus Is Whipped
3. Jesus Is Crowned with Thorns
4. Jesus Carries the Cross
5. Jesus Dies on the Cross

The Glorious Mysteries

1. Jesus Rises from the Dead
2. Jesus Goes Up to Heaven
3. Jesus Sends His Holy Spirit
4. Mary Is Taken to Heaven
5. Mary Is Crowned Queen

1. Make the Sign of the Cross and pray the Apostles' Creed.
2. Pray the Our Father.
3. Pray 3 Hail Marys.
4. Pray the Glory, name the first Mystery, and pray the Our Father.
5. Pray 10 Hail Marys.
6. Pray the Glory, name the second Mystery, and pray the Our Father.
7. Repeat steps 5 and 6 until you reach the end.
8. Pray the Glory and the Hail, Holy Queen. Kiss the crucifix.

BOOKS & MEDIA

The Daughters of St. Paul operate book and media centers
at the following addresses. Visit, call or write the one nearest you today,
or find us on the World Wide Web, www.pauline.org

CALIFORNIA
3908 Sepulveda Blvd, Culver City, CA 90230 — 310-397-8676
2640 Broadway Street, Redwood City, CA 94063 — 650-369-4230
5945 Balboa Avenue, San Diego, CA 92111 — 858-565-9181

FLORIDA
145 S.W. 107th Avenue, Miami, FL 33174 — 305-559-6715

HAWAII
1143 Bishop Street, Honolulu, HI 96813 — 808-521-2731
Neighbor Islands call: — 866-521-2731

ILLINOIS
172 North Michigan Avenue, Chicago, IL 60601 — 312-346-4228

LOUISIANA
4403 Veterans Memorial Blvd, Metairie, LA 70006 — 504-887-7631

MASSACHUSETTS
885 Providence Hwy, Dedham, MA 02026 — 781-326-5385

MISSOURI
9804 Watson Road, St. Louis, MO 63126 — 314-965-3512

NEW JERSEY
561 U.S. Route 1, Wick Plaza, Edison, NJ 08817 — 732-572-1200

NEW YORK
150 East 52nd Street, New York, NY 10022 — 212-754-1110

PENNSYLVANIA
9171-A Roosevelt Blvd, Philadelphia, PA 19114 — 215-676-9494

SOUTH CAROLINA
243 King Street, Charleston, SC 29401 — 843-577-0175

TENNESSEE
4811 Poplar Avenue, Memphis, TN 38117 — 901-761-2987

TEXAS
114 Main Plaza, San Antonio, TX 78205 — 210-224-8101

VIRGINIA
1025 King Street, Alexandria, VA 22314 — 703-549-3806

CANADA
3022 Dufferin Street, Toronto, ON M6B 3T5 — 416-781-9131